Let's visit a
DAIRY FARM

Sarah Doughty
and
Diana Bentley
Reading Consultant
University of Reading

Photographs by
Chris Fairclough

Wayland

Let's Visit a Farm

Beef Farm
Cereal Farm
Dairy Farm
Fish Farm
Fruit Farm
Market Garden
Pig Farm
Poultry Farm
Sheep Farm

First published in 1989 by
Wayland (Publishers) Ltd
61 Western Road, Hove,
East Sussex, BN3 1JD, England

© Copyright 1989 Wayland (Publishers) Ltd

British Library Cataloguing in Publication Data
Doughty, Sarah
  Let's visit a dairy farm.
  1. Dairy farming, — For children
  I. Title   II. Bentley, Diana
  III. Series 636.2'142

ISBN 1–85210–749–9

Phototypeset by
Kalligraphics Ltd
Horley, Surrey
Printed and bound by
Casterman S.A., Belgium

Contents

All the words that appear
in **bold** are explained in the
glossary on page 28.

This is the dairy farm in Devon

Barn

The farm

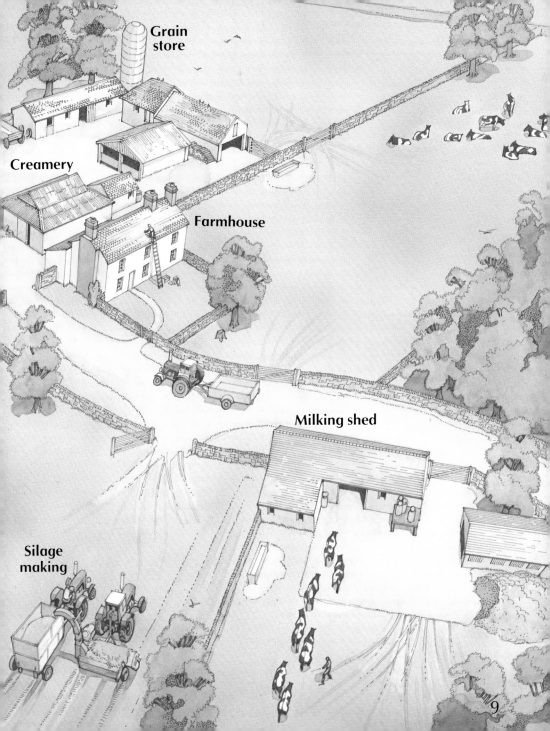

Grain store

Creamery

Farmhouse

Milking shed

Silage making

9

On a dairy farm, the farmer keeps cows

On a dairy farm the farmer keeps cows. Cows give us milk. These cows are black and white. They are called Friesians. Friesian cows give us lots of milk.

Here is the farmer, Mr McKinnon, with some of his friends. George, Joanne and their mother like to help on the farm.

A calf is born

This cow has just had a baby **calf**. The **herdsman** has helped her to give birth. The cow licks her calf clean. Soon the calf will learn to stand up. At first it will be rather wobbly. The calf will be hungry and need to find its mother's milk. The milk she makes contains lots of **nutrients** which will help the calf grow strong.

The calf drinks milk

Mr McKinnon and the herdsman talk to the children. They tell the children how the cow is making milk for her calf. The calf quickly learns to drink milk from the cow's **udder**.

Now the cow is making milk for her calf, the farmer can begin to collect her milk for us to drink. The calf will learn how to drink a milk mixture from a bucket, instead of its mother's milk.

George and Joanne mix the calves' food

Mrs McKinnon shows the children how to mix the calves' food. It is stirred together in buckets. The liquid the calves drink is made up of skimmed milk and vegetable fats. Skimmed milk is ordinary milk with the cream taken off.

17

George and Joanne feed the calves

These calves are a few days old. They are big
enough to be **weaned**. They have been taken away
from their mothers and now live indoors in pens. The
children give the calves the milk mixture to drink
from buckets. Soon the calves will be able to eat
small amounts of solid food. This will be made up of
meal and hay.

The cows go to be milked

These cows have all had calves. They are making lots of milk but they have no calves to feed. Twice a day the cows walk from their field to the milking shed. They like their milking times to be the same every day. The cows go to be milked every morning and evening.

The cows are milked

In the milking shed, a milking machine is used to take milk from a cow. This sucks the milk from her udder. First of all the herdsman cleans the cow's udder. He then attaches four cups which gently suck out the milk. The milk goes into a glass jar. This tells the herdsman how much milk the cow has given. Every cow gives us over seventy pints of milk a day!

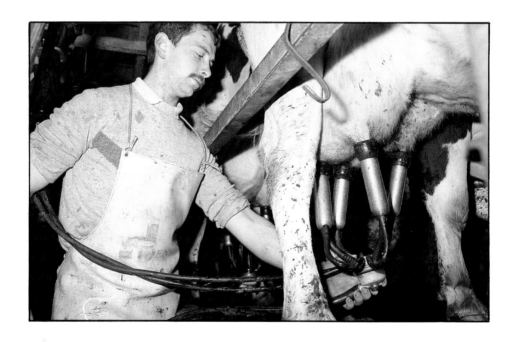

The tanker takes the milk to the local dairy

The milk tanker comes to the farm every day to collect the milk. The milk goes along a pipe into the tanker. The tanker keeps the milk cold and fresh.

At the local dairy the milk is tested to make sure that it is clean. It is heated and then cooled to kill all the germs. This is called pasteurization. The machine you can see here fills thousands of bottles of milk every hour.

25

The milk is made into cheese

On this farm there is a **creamery**. Mr McKinnon uses
some of his cows' milk to make into cheese. The
milk you can see in the **vat** will become solid. This is
done by adding **rennet** to fresh milk. This solid
mixture, called curd, is then put into a mould which
gives the cheese its shape. In a large creamery milk
is also made into butter and cream.

Glossary

Calf A cow's young.

Creamery A place where butter, cream and cheese are made.

Herdsman Person who looks after the herd of cows.

Meal Animal food made from cereals.

Nutrients The goodness in foods.

Rennet A liquid from a calf's stomach used to clot milk.

Udder The part of the cow where milk is made.

Vat A large tank for holding milk.

Weaned When a young animal is given food other than its mother's milk.

Acknowledgement

The publishers would like to thank the dairy farm in association with *Farmer's Weekly* for their help and co-operation in the making of this book.

Books to read

Dairy Cows on the Farm by Cliff Moon (Wayland, 1983)
On the Farm by Sarah McKenzie (Wayland, 1985)
Understanding Farm Animals by Ruth Thomson (Usborne, 1978)

Places to visit

Notes for parents and teachers

To find out more about visiting a dairy farm, or any other type of farm in your area, you might like to get in touch with the following organizations:

The Association of Agriculture (Farm Visits Service), Victoria Chambers, 16–20 Strutton Ground, London SW1P 2HP.
They have produced a useful booklet called *Farms to Visit* which gives details of farms that are open to the public, many with special facilities for schools.

The National Union of Farmers, Agriculture House, 25–31 Knightsbridge, London, SW1 7NJ.
Local branches organize visits to farms. Their addresses can be obtained from your library.

County Colleges of Agriculture
These exist in most counties. Many have an established Schools Liaison or Environmental Studies Unit. Contact the Association of Agriculture if you have difficulty locating your local College of Agriculture.

Index